SENT

Devotions for the Season

SENT

Delivering the Gift of Hope at Christmas

Book
978-1-501-80103-7
978-1-501-80104-4 eBook

Devotions for the Season
978-1-501-80117-4
978-1-501-80118-1 eBook

DVD
978-1-501-80108-2

Leader Guide
978-1-501-80106-8
978-1-501-80107-5 eBook

Youth Study Book
978-1-501-80114-3
978-1-501-80115-0 eBook

Children's Leader Guide
978-1-501-80116-7

For more information, visit www.AbingdonPress.com

SENT

DELIVERING
THE GIFT OF HOPE
AT CHRISTMAS

JORGE ACEVEDO

ith Jacob Armstrong, Rachel Billups, Justin LaRosa & Lanecia Rouse

Abingdon Press
Nashville

Sent
Delivering the Gift of Hope at Christmas
Devotions for the Season

This book is printed on elemental chlorine-free paper.

ISBN 978-1-5018-0117-4

15 16 17 18 19 20 21 22 23 24—10 9 8 7 6 5 4 3 2 1
MANUFACTURED IN THE UNITED STATES OF AMERICA

CONTENTS

INTRODUCTION

Advent is here. These weeks leading to Christmas are a season intended to help us prepare for Jesus' birth. The word *advent* actually means "arrival" or "coming." Yet Jesus' birth is more than a one-time occurrence. How? Every Christmas has within it the possibility of Jesus being born again in our lives and in our world. Historically Jesus' birth happened once, but spiritually his birth can happen anew for us today.

Where does Christ need to be born in you today? One of my mentors, Bishop Dick Wills, used to say that if you can't tell someone what God has done in your life during the last thirty days, you may not have a relationship with God. Dick was arguing for an "up-to-date" faith, a faith constantly being born and reborn in our lives. One of the best ways to cultivate that kind of up-to-date faith is through a regular devotional practice—a time when we meditate on God's Word, reflect on what God is doing in the world and in our lives, and talk with God in prayer.

This book is intended for that purpose—to guide us in a devotional practice during the season of Advent. I have invited four of my friends—Jacob, Lanecia, Justin, and Rachel—to join me in reflecting upon what it means for Jesus to be reborn in our lives. As we explore five themes related to the outcomes of Jesus being born again in our lives, we will prepare spiritually not only for celebrating Jesus' birth, which took place two thousand years ago, but also for inviting his rebirth in our hearts and lives today. As you read, reflect, and pray, remember that just as God sent Jesus to the world so that he might change the world, so you and I are sent into the world to be Jesus' hands and feet today, delivering God's gift of hope to a world in need. It is our prayer that these devotions will help encourage and equip you for that mission.

Jorge Acevedo

WEEK ONE

JESUS RECONCILES

Jacob Armstrong

1. Hold Out Hope

*In the days of King Herod of Judea, there was a priest
named Zechariah, who belonged to the priestly order
of Abijah. His wife was a descendant of Aaron, and
her name was Elizabeth. Both of them were righteous
before God, living blamelessly according to all the
commandments and regulations of the Lord. But they
had no children, because Elizabeth was barren, and they
both were getting on in years. (Luke 1:5-7 NRSV)*

Zechariah and Elizabeth had done it the right way. They
were both "righteous before God" and "living blamelessly
according to all the commandments and regulations of the
Lord" (v. 6). That's just another way of saying that they had
done the right things in the right ways for a long time, and
it didn't pan out for them—at least not in the way or time
they had hoped. Their obedience was not an exemption

from heartache. Their righteous living was not a guarantee that every longing was met. They lived many long years with their longing for children unfulfilled. That's hard—really, really hard.

When we meet Zechariah and Elizabeth, they are old. We don't see their conversations over the years about their inability to have children. We don't see their tears. We don't know who and what they blamed. We are told only that they are old, they have done the right things, and they have no children. No doubt they thought they had missed their chance on many things they had seen their friends and relatives enjoy.

And yet they held out hope—hope in a God who was bigger than their circumstances; hope for a future that was more than they could see and experience. That in itself can be hard as well.

So often things don't go the way I want in the time that I want. Sometimes it's everyday stuff like missing an evening with my family because I can't get home from work. Other times it's bigger than that, such as learning again that I have not measured up professionally or personally or continuing in cycles of anxiety that I can't seem to break. It happens all the time— this life not going as ordered or desired.

When I want to throw in the towel, I am reminded of people like Zechariah and Elizabeth who held out hope. They remind me that I'm not too old for something great to happen. For that matter, I'm not too young, either.

Zechariah and Elizabeth don't give us any reason to take our names off the list of those who can encounter and be used by God. They don't give us permission to allow decade-long disappointments to become reasons to hide our heads in the sand. *Because they held out hope.*

If you have reasons for disqualifying yourself from encountering Jesus in a real, life-changing way, it's time to look at the Christmas story again. If you feel you have missed your chance, remember that God comes in ways we don't expect. Let go of the idea that God has passed you by. The Christmas story gives us no precedent for that kind of thinking. Instead, it begs us to hold out hope as disappointment rears its head again. This Christmas, instead of longing for another present, let's wipe the crust off our aging hearts and continue to long for a God who always holds out hope for us.

Reconciling God, give me strength to face my unmet expectations and disappointments with hope. Remind me that you know and care for me even when I feel as if I've been forgotten. I am looking and listening for you now. Amen.

2. Claimed by God

The angel said to her, "Do not be afraid, Mary, for you have found favor with God." (Luke 1:30 NRSV)

Not far from where I live there is a store that sells unclaimed baggage. These are the suitcases, duffel bags, and other packages that were left on lonely baggage claim conveyor belts and never picked up. They served their time at the airport, patiently waiting for their owners to return, but they were never claimed. Thousands and thousands of bags arrive at the store, and their contents are sold at discount prices. It is a strange sight, really—all these items that once belonged to people now forgotten and left behind.

I often am surprised by how many people I talk to who don't feel much different than these discarded suitcases. People who, from my vantage point, are beautiful, successful, talented, and intelligent can feel very little worth. I talked recently with a friend I have admired for many years, and as he talked I couldn't believe what a skewed view of himself he has. He is amazing, but he can't see it—at least he couldn't then. But it's not just other people. I am surprised how often I can feel less than and insecure—and I just plain know better.

I love how the angel spoke to Mary. His first words to her were, "You have found favor with God" (Luke 1:30 NRSV). In other words, you have great worth to God. God has chosen you. Then the angel urged her not to be afraid. God, the angel said, is honoring you.

We are familiar with Mary, the mother of Jesus, being honored. She is one of the most revered figures in human history. But she must have thought, "Me? Highly favored? God is honoring me?" Mary first gave some reasons why this couldn't be so, but then she accepted it. She accepted that she was favored or honored by God.

This story shouldn't cause us to see Mary as superhuman or as one among a group of rare individuals God desires. Instead, her normalcy and humble disposition should lead us to see ourselves. And as we see ourselves in her ordinariness, we then must open our hearts to hear God call us favored and honored.

I wish I could relive that conversation with my friend. I would grab him by the arm and say, "You are loved and favored by God."

Don't be afraid; God is looking to honor you by including you in the great story of reconciliation. If you feel like unclaimed baggage today—going round and round on the conveyor belt, overlooked and unwanted—try to stop and hear God's words of worth. They aren't just for Mary; they are for you too.

God, today when I feel insecure, please remind me of my great worth to you. When I feel ordinary, remind me that is precisely the kind of person you desire and use. When I feel unclaimed, assure me of the claim you have on me. Amen.

3. Flip the Script

*Just when he had resolved to do this, an angel of the Lord
appeared to him in a dream and said, "Joseph, son of
David, do not be afraid to take Mary as your wife, for the
child conceived in her is from the Holy Spirit."*
(Matthew 1:20 NRSV)

One of the things I love to do this time of year is watch
classic Christmas movies.

In *How the Grinch Stole Christmas*, the Grinch's heart
is three sizes too small; so he sneaks into Who-ville in the
middle of the night and steals all the Christmas presents—not
only the presents but also the decorations, the trees, and the
roast beast. The next morning Who-ville awakens to find that
everything representing Christmas is gone.

In *A Christmas Story*, young Ralphie has been dreaming
of one thing alone: a Red Ryder BB gun. He wakes up on

Christmas morning and unwraps two presents, only to discover socks and a pink bunny costume. And he's even forced to put on the costume.

In *It's a Wonderful Life*, George Bailey's Christmas is even worse. After a major financial disaster at the building and loan he manages, he thinks his family would be better off without him. So he goes to the edge of town to jump off a bridge. He's ready to end it all and wishes he was never born, but then an angel grants his wish and shows him what life what would have been like without him. He realizes the impact he had on others and wants to return to his life, but he's afraid it may be too late.

As I recount each plot, we can grin and even feel a sense of excitement because we know that's not how the story ends. We know the ending, and so we anticipate what is coming next.

In each movie, the writers flip the script just when we can't take it anymore. The Grinch hears the Whos singing, his heart begins to grow, and Christmas is restored. Ralphie's dad motions him toward one more gift behind the tree—one even mom doesn't know about—and he unwraps the Red Ryder BB gun. The whole town shows up at George Bailey's home with money to pay the debt he owes, showing that they believe in him. A bell rings, and an angel gets his wings.

Every good Christmas movie has the element of some deep longing that is not only met but also exceeded. Why? Because the first Christmas story is full of such moments. God is in the business of flipping scripts that seemed doomed for despair.

Joseph's dreams are crushed when he learns that his fiancée, Mary, is pregnant and the child is not his. All his plans come crashing to the ground. Joseph plans to divorce her quietly and pick up the pieces of his life. Then God flips the script.

In a dream an angel tells Joseph that the child is from God and that he will be the one who saves his people from their sins. Didn't see that coming.

So, when all the gifts are stolen (even the tree and the roast beast); when the gifts are opened and you are left wearing a bunny suit; when you've lost your business, your family, and your history—remember that God is waiting to speak to you in a dream and reconcile the things that are broken, making them whole again. It's what God does. God reconciles us and then sends us into his story to help reconcile others.

God, when everything seems headed for disaster, remind me that you are with me and can make a way when I can't. Give me trust, hope, and anticipation of the good you can make of my messes. Amen.

4. We Still Need Jesus

Then was fulfilled what had been spoken through the prophet Jeremiah:

> *A voice was heard in Ramah,*
> *wailing and loud lamentation,*
> *Rachel weeping for her children;*
> *she refused to be consoled, because they are*
> *no more."*

(Matthew 2:17-18 NRSV)

I reluctantly walked into the gym, stepped onto the treadmill, put my headphones in my ears, and tried to start Monday off right. As I began to walk, I connected the headphones to the treadmill and selected one of the TV screens in front of me. Before I could even turn the sound up, my eyes were drawn to a breaking news banner on the bottom of the screen. It said that 126 were dead in a school shooting.

I took a breath and wiped the sleep out of my eyes. I stopped the treadmill. The audio in my ears told me the beginning details of a brutal massacre in Pakistan.

At the same time a moving scroller on the bottom of the TV screen announced that a school system in Pennsylvania was shut down because an armed man was on the loose.

Almost simultaneously my phone vibrated with a message giving details about a memorial service for a beloved teacher in our community who had died after a valiant fight with cancer. She left behind her husband and two boys. We would hold the service in the gym of the school where she taught and where our church worships.

It was the week before Christmas, and that night I was planning to attend yet another festive holiday celebration. I was supposed to feel cheery, but I wanted to take my earphones out, close my eyes, and throw my phone across the room. Yet I know as well as you do that you can't close your eyes and ears well enough to shut out the pain of this world.

It helps me to remember that the world Jesus entered was not unlike ours. In fact, the first Christmas took place in a time when innocent children were being killed. The first Christmas took place in a time when evil men did evil things. The first Christmas took place during a week when all in the community were crying together. The world needed Jesus then, and we still need Jesus now.

We usually skip over this verse in the Christmas story about children being killed and mothers weeping for their children, but it's there. When Herod realized that he had been outwitted by the magi, he was furious and gave orders to kill all the boys in Bethlehem and the vicinity who were two years old and under. It is a terrible scene in the Christmas story, but it is a part of the story nonetheless.

We can't forget that Jesus came into a world in desperate need not only of a beautiful scene but also of a savior. Jesus was sent to reconcile broken hearts and broken people in a broken world. We don't have to look far to be reminded that our world is broken. Thanks be to God that Jesus has come to us and will come again.

Today as we remember how Jesus was sent to us, let us consider to whom we are being sent as his messengers.

God, I am so grateful that you hear my weeping and grieving. Thank you for sending Jesus into the world to meet each one of us in our brokenness. I need him today. Amen.

5. Jesus Is Sent for All

The angel said to them, "Do not be afraid; for see—I am bringing you good news of great joy for all the people."
(Luke 2:10 NRSV)

I often wonder about the word *all* in this verse. God's good news is good news of great joy for *all* people. At first it seems easy to believe the good news is for all people; but when we look at the way most of us dole out love and mercy, we must admit we're really quite selective with it. The truth is that it's hard to believe the good news is for everybody. In fact, it's overwhelming to consider it.

It reminds me of the times when my wife comes into the living room after I have been playing with my three daughters. Let me set the scene. We have the Legos out, and we are eating popcorn. A fort has been built out of couch cushions, and there are some items scattered on the floor that were displaced when we were wrestling near the coffee table. We've read some books and done a little homework, and there is evidence that some leftover Halloween candy has been eaten. It probably has taken us only twenty minutes to create this scene. Then in walks Rachel, and she pronounces, "All right, guys, we have to pick all this stuff up."

Immediately we want to know what she means by *all*.

You mean the Legos and the popcorn? Yes. And the couch-cushion fort? Yes. And the mess from wrestling? Yes. The books? The homework? The candy wrappers? Yes, yes, yes. We realize that when she said *all* this stuff, what she meant was *all* this stuff. It's a little overwhelming. *All* is overwhelming.

In God's story we hear that the good news of reconciliation is for all the people, and we wonder what God means by *all*.

The people who look like us? Yes. The people who don't? Yes. The old people who seem to have been passed by? Yes. The pregnant teenage moms? Yes. The young men who have a plan but then life takes a crazy turn? Yes. The rich folks who seem to have it all figured out but are dying on the inside? Yes. The working folks, such as third-shift shepherds? Yes.

The good news of reconciliation is for *all* of these people. We look at one another and realize that what God meant by *all* was *all*, and it is a little overwhelming. But it is good news!

God has good news of great joy to share, and it is for everybody. On the first Christmas, the message was shouted from the skies, and we should shout it too. Amazingly, the way

God gets the message out is through us. We become like the angels in the story who go and tell all the people that Jesus has come—for *all*. Jesus was sent into the world to reconcile all people to God, and we are being sent into the world to share this message with all the people God puts before us.

Where is God sending you today? To whom is God sending you?

Send me, O God, with the good news of great joy of this season—the news of reconciliation. Jesus has come and is coming. May I join the angels in proclaiming it to all the people you put before me. Amen.

WEEK TWO

JESUS SETS US FREE

Lanecia Rouse

6. Already Good

The Lord is the Spirit, and where the Lord's Spirit is,
there is freedom. All of us are looking with unveiled faces
at the glory of the Lord as if we were looking in a mirror.
We are being transformed into that same image from one
degree of glory to the next degree of glory. This comes from
the Lord, who is the Spirit.

(2 Corinthians 3:17-18 CEB)

"Look at that cup, Sunshine! What do you think of it?"
I said this because I was delighted to see the clay artwork my
friend was creating. I remembered the day Sunshine would
not even consider participating in the art classes we offered
at the shelter, and now she was sitting at the table next to me,
making pottery to sell.

"Well, you know," she responded with a modest smile
and giggle, "I think it's all right. The bottom is a little uneven
around the edges. It's good, though."

"Oh, I bet the teacher can help you fix that," I replied, and I invited the pottery teacher over to help make the bottom of the cup just *perfect*. Like any good teacher, she began offering Sunshine ways she could smooth out the edge with a little water, a sponge, and time. I added a bit of my knowledge as well. Sunshine extended such grace and patience to us as she listened and affirmed our words with a nod.

Once we finished, Sunshine gently said, "Oh, no. I mean, I like it, because I made it. You know?" The cup in her hand belonged to her, and before it was even finished she already loved and accepted it. There was nothing we could have taught her about making the cup better that would have made Sunshine love the cup more.

As Sunshine continued to create, I pondered her words. Eventually she wrote the word *love* and John 3:16—her favorite Scripture—on the cup, and she told us with delight that it was finished, rugged edges and all. It was indeed finished. It was beautiful and identifiably hers to those of us who knew her.

Perhaps the invitation for us this Advent is to trust and walk in the Spirit of Christ and the liberating good news that we are accepted and loved by God even before we are finished. Christ invites us to a new way of being. Often, however, we don't enjoy our walk in Christ because we are hindered by rigorous human standards that misrepresent God's view of us as "already good" because God made us.

Maybe this Advent we, like Sunshine, should see ourselves through this Spirit of truth, which frees us to live life with joy and true liberty.

Creating and re-creating God, touch my eyes that I may truly see my neighbors and myself as accepted and loved by you already. Free me from those things that hinder me from walking freely in the light of this love. May I be confident that as you complete your work in me, I am already good in your sight through Christ. Amen.

7. Agents of Love

"Then those who are righteous will reply to him, 'Lord, when did we see you hungry and feed you, or thirsty and give you a drink? When did we see you as a stranger and welcome you, or naked and give you clothes to wear? When did we see you sick or in prison and visit you?'
"Then the king will reply to them, 'I assure you that when you have done it for one of the least of these brothers and sisters of mine, you have done it for me.'"

(Matthew 25:37-40 CEB)

One summer a youth group began a Bible study journey together in hopes of discerning how God was calling them to be agents of love in their city. They spent the summer practicing *lectio divina*, or "divine reading," with Matthew 25:37-40 each week. This practice, they prayed, would grant clarity to them as they "joined Jesus in mission" over the next year. They studied the Scriptures together, engaged in conversations with people in the community, and sought to hear and understand the various needs of the city. After much prayer, listening, and conversation, they decided to be intentional about welcoming and cultivating friendships with a group of children and youth in their church seeking refuge in the city from what is known as the Golden Triangle of Asia.

The youth group decided that the best place to start was fellowship, cultivating genuine relationships with the children and youth from Asia. Over the next few months, the youth began to organize parties and play opportunities for everyone. These parties led to other days of fun at their homes away from church, where everyone played soccer, created art, and shared stories about life and faith together.

The intentional times spent together, entering into one another's stories and discovering needs, led to a quality summer camp experience, which included sports, arts, education tutorials, and Bible study for children who could not otherwise afford it. It also gave birth to summer tutoring programs, which were needed when funding cuts for summer school impacted class availability. In short, friendships were formed and God was able to create something beautiful in the lives of all involved—all because the youth took time to study, pray, pay attention, listen, and commit to join God where God was at work.

Sometimes joining God's mission does not look as we thought it would. As the Scriptures reveal to us, we often encounter Christ in the most unlikely places. When the summer Bible study youth group was able to break free of social, economic, and cultural barriers and enter into authentic friendships with their neighbors, they exhibited the reconciling power of the love of God. In such cases, the lines between those serving and those being served become blurry, and we are able to become co-creators with God, bringing restoration, light, and hope to one another.

God, touch my eyes that I may see you in my neighbor. Open my ears that I may hear the needs and tears of others and then, without fear, respond with the love I have come to know through Jesus Christ. Work in and through me that I may be a bearer of your love and hope to all. Amen.

8. More Than Enough

Taking them with him, Jesus withdrew privately to a city called Bethsaida. When the crowds figured it out, they followed him. He welcomed them, spoke to them about God's kingdom, and healed those who were sick. When the day was almost over, the Twelve came to him and said, "Send the crowd away so that they can go to the nearby villages and countryside and find lodging and food, because we are in a deserted place." He replied, "You give them something to eat." But they said, "We have no more than five loaves of bread and two fish—unless we go and buy food for all these people."...He took the five loaves and the two fish, looked up to heaven, blessed them, and broke them and gave them to the disciples to set before the crowd. Everyone ate until they were full, and the disciples filled twelve baskets with the leftovers.

(Luke 9:10-13, 16-17 CEB)

One time a friend invited me to coffee to catch up on life. During the conversation, he told me about things that were weighing heavy on him about his sense of call to serve in a community where there were great needs. He believed he had good ideas about how to address one of these needs in particular; however, he was feeling mentally fatigued and stretched by carrying a few heavy burdens of his own and was unsure if he had enough material and spiritual resources to say yes to the task. After a few months, my friend decided to say yes anyway. As he ignored his insufficiency, shared his vision, and started in the work, he found that he and God were more than enough to do what was required. Things started to fall into place as others came alongside to help shape the vision and support the work with unique gifts and resources.

Like my friend, we can wrestle with feelings of emotional fatigue, spiritual anxiety, and material limitations. Today's Scripture passage shows us that these feelings arise naturally out of our shared human experience.

Preceding this passage is the story of John the Baptist's beheading. Jesus seemed to be deeply grieved by the news of John's death and departed to a solitary place, no doubt to mourn and seek spiritual renewal in prayer. Even so, Jesus couldn't get away. Crowds of people followed him, and the disciples were there with their own complaints and worries. It would be understandable if Jesus became frustrated. Despite his own grief, he still had persons pressing him to meet *their* needs, and his disciples were exhausted and irritated because they realized their own sense of limitation. They expressed this irritation when they said to Jesus, "Let's send the people away. We only have five fish and some loaves left!" Jesus' response was quite instructive. Instead of being exasperated, he showed compassion, freeing the disciples from a perspective of lack and encouraging them to realize that they had more than enough to meet the need.

Jesus helped the disciples first by having them grapple with what they *could do*: "You feed them," he said. Jesus wanted them to see that such a calling required faith, not fear and avoidance of responsibility. It required that they creatively think of solutions, as best as they could, and trust God for the rest. Next, Jesus told his disciples to give to him what they did have. He blessed the offering and began feeding the crowd, not thinking about the limits of supply. And as the story goes, there was more than enough. Jesus taught his disciples through this experience that by giving what you *do* have and not worrying about your limitations, you can witness the miraculous.

As we follow Jesus, there will be times when we are overwhelmed and depleted. Even when we are grieving, tired, and unable to see all the possibilities, there may be unfair expectations. In such times, we can be assured that God knows our constraints and will work with what we *do* have to offer. And as my friend discovered, we will find that we are enough.

May you live in the liberating perspective that *you are enough*.

Lord, you command us to love you with our whole being and to love our neighbors as ourselves. I confess that at times this can be overwhelming, and I'm not always sure I have what it takes to do what is loving, just, and kind. When those times come, liberate me from a perspective of lack and enable me to live out a perspective shaped by love, hope, and faith—faith that there are always enough resources to love my neighbor. Amen.

9. Light in the Darkness

The light shines in the darkness,
and the darkness doesn't extinguish the light.
(John 1:5 CEB)

December 4, 2013, will forever be imprinted upon my heart. That day my water broke and I gave birth to my twenty-two-week-old baby girl, Annĕe. I spent hours in labor, hoping against what all the doctors knew would be inevitable. And within two hours of taking her first breath, she died, resting in the loving embrace of her mother and father. Only three days before we had been with our church family preparing for Advent, and now death, darkness, loss, and grief blanketed us. Our hearts were shattered.

The world seemed to be basking in the light and joyful wonder that the season brings, but not me. I sat still in the shadow of my baby's death, fighting hard not to drown in an ocean of tears and shipwrecked dreams. To welcome her life and then watch it slip away within two hours was surreal and incredibly traumatic. In the face of such unimaginable pain that first night in the hospital, I found myself wondering, at times wailing, "How am I ever going to get through this? God where are you? Where are you *now*?"

As we journey through our grief, God's responses to our cries are not always grand or easily identifiable. However, I knew the only way I could survive this "new normal" was to keep looking for God. In order for me not only to survive but to live with the pain of this heartbreak, it was essential for me to keep looking for Love to meet me in the dark. I longed for God to be close, yet God felt so far.

In the following months I waited for the reality of the song lyric, "Night has always pushed up day,"[1] and I kept watch for Emmanuel—God with us. There were moments during the early stages of grief when God's loving presence with me was undeniable. My family and friends became light-bearers for me as they visited us in the hospital and at home, sat with us in our grief during our daughter's memorial service, provided meals for us, helped me fulfill work obligations, sent care packages, and created space for us to be.

There also were many moments when I had to fight to see Love with me; it was faint through my veil of tears. Yet Love did show up—in silence, in the tender embrace of my husband, and in a random phone call from someone who reached out, not knowing it was the moment I needed it the most. In those moments, the light of Christ penetrated through the darkest of nights, freeing me to see and embrace a hope beyond my situation. They offered the comfort and connection I needed to have the strength to navigate through that very long night and live into the dawning of a new day.

Advent is the season of light, but it also can be a time of darkness for those who are hurting. If you are experiencing a dark night, hold on to the promise that Love will meet you where you are, penetrating the darkness with the light of Christ. And if you are basking in the light and joyful wonder of the season, remember to be a light-bearer to those who may be struggling.

God, be with me from dawn to dusk to dawn again. By your light, help me to navigate through the pain and suffering of life without being overcome. Help me be a light-bearer to those who need someone to guide them through their own dark nights. Amen.

1. Mumford and Sons. "After the Storm." *Sigh No More.* Universal Music Publishing Group, 2009. CD.

10. Sing Your Song

I will sing to the LORD as long as I live;
I will sing praises to my GOD while I'm still alive.
(Psalm 104:33 CEB)

It was a Sunday during Advent, and I and the other choir members were making our procession down the center aisle of the sanctuary when I looked out the open front door to see a friend stumbling up the white stone steps of the church. My friend Steve, who loves music and sings very well, had woken up from a cold concrete bed a few streets away and decided that he wanted to attend worship. It was the first time in a long time I'd seen Steve on a Sunday morning. We typically saw him during the week when he would come with his buddies to the church for assistance, a snack bag, or just conversation. But this Sunday morning he was alone, visibly intoxicated, and eager to get inside.

Because of my worship leadership responsibilities that particular morning, I immediately found my sister, Ciona, and let her know that Steve was coming up the stairs. She and Steve had been friends for a while too, and there was evident love between them. She walked out, greeted him, and invited him to sit next to her. As they sat, he shared with her that he had come to sing a particular song. Despite the restraints of the order of worship printed in the bulletin, he was intent on getting the choir to sing that song.

As the service progressed, he became more demanding and disruptive. He kept asking Ciona when he could walk up to the front and ask the choir director for the song, "The Little Drummer Boy." It was difficult for him to accept that there was no room in the service for his request, and he struggled to suppress his feelings. A bit heartbroken, Ciona asked Steve if they could go outside to sing his song and chat for a bit.

As they sat outside, Steve began to cry, preach, and stumble through his song. He looked at her as he sang, "Come they told me, pa rum pum pum pum / A newborn King to see, pa rum pum pum pum." He continued, singing the song by heart. When he finished, he shared words about his love for Jesus and walked away.

Steve's intentions that day were to bring a gift. It was a gift of remembering that Jesus came so we might know that we all are invited to come, that we all have a song to sing, and that Jesus makes space for everyone to sing his or her own song. It reminded me that following the way of Jesus means not only singing my song but also affirming the gifts that every single person has to offer God—regardless of life circumstances—for the sake of love and the restoration of wholeness for ourselves and the world. This is the good news—the freeing, healing and empowering news—that Jesus came to bring.

The gift Steve gave through his willingness and determination to sing his song to the Lord that morning was one of the best Christmas gifts I have ever received. What is your song to sing this Advent?

Creating and re-creating God, thank you for sending Jesus to offer and embody for the world a new song that we all can choose to sing in our own ways. Teach me how to sing your song in the unique way you've given me to sing it, participating fully with my heart, mind, and soul. As I sing, mold and shape me to create spaces of hospitality and unconditional love in my life so that I may welcome my neighbors, listen to them sing their songs, and encourage them along the way. Amen.

WEEK THREE
JESUS IS GOD WITH US

Justin LaRosa

11. "God With Us" Always

"The virgin will conceive and give birth to a son, and they will call him Immanuel" (which means "God with us"). (Matthew 1:23 NIV)

God came to humanity through Jesus of Nazareth. It's quite shocking, really. The Hebrew people were expecting a powerful Messiah who would restore the kingdom of Israel, but Jesus ushered in a different kind of kingdom—one not built upon power, prestige, and possession but upon powerless love. It was surprising and shocking—not at all what they expected.

If we're honest, we're often surprised and shocked by the way that Jesus comes to us too. He can be hidden in plain sight, showing up in ways we never anticipated. Just when circumstances appear to be at their bleakest, Jesus reveals himself and gives us new life. That's the way it was for me.

I have always believed in God, but my circumstances and environment when I was growing up were catalysts for shaping the notion that God was indifferent. I saw God as the Creator who sat back and watched but didn't intervene. I also had serious doubts about Christianity's claims in regard to Jesus—that he was "God with us" sent to redeem, sustain, and make everything new.

Throughout my childhood, teenage years, and young adulthood, there were a variety of factors that shaped my intense faith struggle, but there were two major life events that set a cast around my heart that would be hard to break. The first is one of my earliest and most vivid childhood memories. At just over three years old, I was informed that my biological father was leaving our family. He bent down to tell me goodbye with tears in his eyes, and then he walked out the door. I remember seeing my mother's sad but stoic expression as she stood motionless next to the front door with her arms rigidly crossed. When the door closed, the abandonment reverberated in my soul.

The second event occurred when I was almost ten years old and my grandparents moved away to Florida. They were the ones who had rooted me in love and faith (which would enable me to return to the faith many years later). Each week until I was nine they had taken me to Sunday Mass and Wednesday programming at the Catholic church. They were a stabilizing and loving force in my chaotic home life. I

45

anticipated our weekends together and our routine of Friday spaghetti dinners with ice cream, fun-filled Saturday activities, and Sunday Mass. So on that crisp day in October as I watched the back of the U-Haul fade into the distance, any hope in a loving God vanished. It was an image that would solidify my understandable but erroneous perception that God is *not* with us.

These two early life events watered seeds of doubt regarding a loving, relational God. My intense feelings of disconnection led to drug and alcohol addiction. Life was filled with emptiness, ruin, and devastating consequences.

But one day God's searching love shattered my Jesus paradigm. Being part of the fellowship of a twelve-step recovery group, recommitting my life to following Jesus in community, and gaining a new perspective on those life-altering events gave me new life. I discovered that God had never abandoned me. In fact, I now could see all the points along the way where Jesus had been with me, including when my father and grandparents left. No longer was I a victim of my past hurts and transgressions. As I grew in community, God's grace reclaimed and reshaped my perception, understanding, and experience of Jesus. I came to see and believe that Jesus was, indeed, "God with us."

Is Jesus hidden in plain sight in your life? Ask him to open your eyes so that you may see and believe he is "God with us"—always.

God of love, I give thanks that you are a God of presence. Give me eyes to see that you are hidden in plain sight—in my past, present, and future. May I continue to grow in the knowledge and love of Jesus Christ—God with us, now and forever. Amen.

12. "God With Us" in Our Pain

When Jesus saw her weeping, and the Jews who had come
along with her also weeping, he was deeply moved in
spirit and troubled. . . . Jesus wept.

(John 11:33, 35 NIV)

Most of us have aspects of our lives, whether past or present, that we would prefer to remain in the darkness and shadows. Depending on the secret, we may go to great lengths to conceal or forget it.

I remember meeting with a friend I had come to know through the twelve-step program. We met in a local park so that I could listen to his story, which was related to the written inventory of the fourth step. Sharing the inventory is similar to the Catholic tradition of reconciliation in which you confess your sins to another person, thereby pulling the sins out of the shadows and into the light. Persons completing the fourth step must catalog the resentments they hold in their hearts toward others, list the ways in which they participated or nurtured those resentments, write any fears they have, and painstakingly inventory their past sinful conduct. It is not for the faint of heart!

I had known this friend for several years and knew that he had significant pain and wreckage in his past. I sensed it because he carried his mistrust, apprehension, and pain in his demeanor. As a result, he had major uneasiness with regard to God and difficulty staying sober. After sitting down and saying a prayer, I remarked, "Why don't you start with something that you either weren't planning on telling me or that you were going to save for last?"

Silence ensued.

He went on to expose a number of deep, painful violations and memories that he had never shared with anyone. As he recounted his stories, he reluctantly shed tears of pain, grief, and anger that had been bottled up for years.

It isn't easy shining a light in darkness, especially on the secrets in our own lives. The journeys of our lives mandate that we encounter, engage, and navigate pain. We create pain, and we receive pain. We can't escape it, despite our efforts to stuff it. That's what was happening with my friend. He had stuffed his pain deep inside, and that day it was boiling over—pain that was fracturing his relationships with God, himself, and many others around him.

Though the pain and grief we experience varies in kind and degree, the fact is that we all have it. Whether it comes from others, our own actions, or unavoidable life circumstances that are nobody's fault, pain is part of the human experience. Regardless of our backgrounds or experiences, shining a light on our pain is an important step in our transformation. If we don't allow God to transform our pain, we surely will project it onto others.

Today's Scripture is simple and profound. Jesus was deeply moved and troubled by the grief of Mary and those gathered to mourn the death of her brother—and his friend—Lazarus. His response was to identify and enter their pain.

Jesus was sent to be God with us in our pain. He was sent for Mary and her friends. He was sent for my friend. He was sent for me. He was sent for *you*. Allow him to enter your pain today.

God of light, shine your grace, mercy, and love in the places of my pain—and the places of pain for all those of this world. Give each of us the wisdom to know how to allow you to transform our pain. Amen.

13. "God With Us" in Our Waiting

"Be still, and know that I am God." (Psalm 46:10 NIV)

Waiting is difficult. Early in our marriage, my wife and I became friends with a couple who had a strong desire to become parents but were struggling to conceive. We were in our late twenties, and they were in their early thirties. They had been married just a few years longer than we had. They told us how they watched as, one by one, their family, friends, neighbors, and acquaintances all had children. While they shared in the joy of those embarking on parenthood, witnessing others having the opportunity to become parents re-exposed their wound of not being able to conceive. They, too, were intentionally trying to conceive. They were faithful in prayer. They were faithful to their church.

Days turned into months, and months turned into a couple of years. They waited and prayed. They visited doctors, ran tests, prayed some more, and asked others to pray. Still nothing. A couple of years turned into nine long years. It seemed like every time they picked up the paper or saw the news, they would see stories about parents who abused their children or who appeared to be ill-equipped for the job of parenting. They dutifully attended the birthday parties of their friends' children year after year, because they wanted to be present and supportive. But the reality was that it incited their longing and picked at their fears and hurts. Both of them began to have seeds of bitterness toward God and their friends, even though they resisted those feelings. They viewed their prayers as fruitless, not just because they weren't getting what they desired but because it felt as though God was absent. There was dryness and distance in their relationship with Jesus. But they kept waiting—privately and in community.

For our friends, it became more and more difficult to trust in God, especially as time marched on and they experienced disconnection in their relationship with God. Both remained faithful. But living today's Scripture, Psalm 46:10, is easier said than done.

Most of us have experienced disconnection with God at one time or another in our lives. Perhaps you were waiting for an important shift to occur and God seemed to go radio silent. Or perhaps you were waiting for a relationship to change, a loved one to be healed, someone to surrender an addiction, a loved one to get better, or a child to be conceived.

If none of these descriptions fits you, you probably will have the opportunity to wait at a later time.

Jesus is "God with us" in the waiting—no matter what we are waiting for. Jesus is with us in our perceived connection and disconnection—in silence and in noise.

Cultivating stillness can help us have the right spirit as we wait. One avenue is to cultivate interior stillness through a practice of silence. Prayer without words cultivates relationship with Jesus. Using methods such as centering prayer or the Jesus prayer ("Lord Jesus Christ, Son of God, have mercy on me, a sinner") deepens our relationship with Christ.

Stillness is one faithful way to wait upon God. So today, be still and know.

God, I lift you the prayers of my heart. Help me to be aware of the ways in which you are waiting with me, my family, my community, and the world. Help me to be present to the people in my life who are waiting and need someone to wait with them; in Christ's name I pray. Amen.

14. "God With Us" in Times of Rejoicing

"Suppose one of you has a hundred sheep and loses one
of them. Doesn't he leave the ninety-nine in the open
country and go after the lost sheep until he finds it?
And when he finds it, he joyfully puts it on his shoulders
and goes home. Then he calls his friends and neighbors
together and says, 'Rejoice with me; I have found my lost
sheep.' I tell you that in the same way there will be more
rejoicing in heaven over one sinner who repents than over
ninety-nine righteous persons who do not need to repent."
(Luke 15:4-7 NIV)

I have had a number of good dogs in my life, all of whom I have loved. But my current dog is something special. His name is Karl, and he's a Shepherd /Lab mix that we rescued. He's friendly, sweet, super smart, obedient, great with kids, submissive (in a good way), and gentle. He tries to befriend even the fussiest of dogs. To give you an idea of what an extraordinary dog he is, my close friend who is a vet remarks that Karl is one of the three best dogs he has ever met.

Toward the end of the day, Karl makes his way to the front door, waiting for the rumble of my truck to come toward the house. When he hears it, he squeaks with delight. Once I'm home, he rarely leaves my side; he's my shadow wherever I go. If these reasons weren't enough for me to love him, Karl is the only living being in my house that actually listens to me. That's a joke—kind of.

Did I mention that I love this dog?

One morning I woke up particularly early, and something was different. Karl was not sitting at my feet trying to lick me. He wasn't banging the wall with his wagging tail. He was nowhere to be found. He was lost.

I replayed in my mind the prior evening, reconstructing what must have happened. My heart sank as I recalled that at 11:00 p.m. I went out to my truck without closing the house door behind me. Karl must have followed me out of the house. I went back into the house not knowing that he was outside.

When I came to that realization, I searched the house inside and out. We contacted neighbors and animal services. We posted a notice on social media. We posted flyers throughout the neighborhood. As I was stapling a flyer on a telephone pole, I was overcome with the notion that I might not see Karl again. It was an emotional moment.

I just wasn't going to give up. So I combed the neighborhood on a bicycle, calling out his name. Then I drove around in the car. I returned to the house mentally and emotionally exhausted.

As I was walking up to our front door, I was overcome. There was Karl. Thankfully, someone in the neighborhood had returned him. There aren't words to express the joy and gratitude that I experienced in that moment! Somehow having lost him deepened my experience of having him back. And when I shared the news with family, neighbors, the online community, and even strangers, they all celebrated. The joy of finding Karl had a ripple effect.

In a small way, losing Karl, searching for Karl, finding Karl, and rejoicing over having Karl again is similar to the story of the lost sheep in today's Scripture. Jesus is the loving shepherd who will go to any lengths to find one of his sheep. And when he finds it, he joyfully puts it on his shoulders, takes it home, and throws a party!

Sometimes we are like the lost sheep, and Jesus searches for us and rejoices when we are found. Other times we are like the shepherd; we are the one throwing a party when we have great cause for rejoicing. Either way, Jesus is there in the midst of the joy. He rejoices for us, and he rejoices with us.

As we celebrate Jesus' birth this Christmas, may we remember that he is "God with us" in times of rejoicing.

God of searching love, today I pray for the parts of me that have gone astray and for the people in my life who seem to be lost and hurting. I give thanks that you not only search for us until you find us; you throw a party when we are found! And I give thanks that when we are filled with joy, you celebrate with us. Thank you for being "God with us" in times of rejoicing. Amen.

15. Sent to Be God With Others

*"You are the light of the world. A town built on a hill
cannot be hidden. Neither do people light a lamp and
put it under a bowl. Instead they put it on its stand, and
it gives light to everyone in the house. In the same way,
let your light shine before others, that they may see your
good deeds and glorify your Father in heaven."*
(Matthew 5:14-16 NIV)

The mental chatter in my head was loud as I sat impatiently
on one of the many uncomfortable, plastic chairs arranged in
a circle. I was at the local jail in a sterile, halogen-lit classroom
with lots of windows. Soon several sheriff deputies would
arrive, escorting somewhere between twelve to twenty men
from different areas of the jail. They were coming to participate
in an eight-week parenting class that I had put together and
was scheduled to facilitate.

I knew to some degree what to expect. The deputies would arrive, get the men situated, and then depart, locking the door behind them. Then they would retreat to a nearby office.

There I sat, a young guy in his mid-twenties (who looked even younger) doing something way out of his comfort zone. Not yet having children of my own, I didn't have a clue about how to parent, but I did know what it was like not to have a dad around; and I felt called to do something about it. I had been sent to be with absent fathers in a place I never would have predicted.

Make no mistake about it, *you* are sent too—sent to be a light to the world. That means you are sent to be Jesus' love to others, even when that may call you to people or places that are foreign or uncomfortable. I don't know about you, but I prefer to feel confident and capable when I am embarking on new ways of serving. Yet it has been said that God doesn't call the qualified; God qualifies the called.

Throughout the Bible we see people who were afraid of God's call. They often resisted before being sent to people, situations, and circumstances that required them to trust in God rather than in their abilities. Just like the prophets, disciples, and others in Scripture, we too are usually called to anything but comfort. But we can find comfort in knowing that we are never alone.

Advent is a time to remember the gift of Jesus. Jesus is "God with us" *always*—in our pain, in our waiting, in times of rejoicing. It is my prayer that our pain, waiting, and joy will be fertile breeding grounds for God's call, leading us to go and make God's love real in meaningful and faithful ways. As we remember and live out the reality that Jesus is "God with us" always, until the end of the age, may God's light radiate through us in the darkest of places.

Jesus, thank you for being "God with us"—at all times and in all places. You have sent me to be a light to the world—to share your love with my family, friends, strangers, and even enemies. Sometimes this calls me out of my comfort zone and way beyond my own abilities. So once again I let go and put my trust in you. May I never forget that you are with me—always. Amen.

WEEK FOUR

JESUS BRINGS NEW LIFE

Rachel Billups

16. Dry Bones

He asked me, "Son of man, can these bones live?"
I said, "Sovereign LORD, you alone know."
(Ezekiel 37:3 NIV)

As I was standing in the sanctuary, Marsha took me aside and reassured me that nothing was going to change at this church. "It has been this way for the last twenty-five years, and it will be this way for the next," she said. All of my youthful optimism was useless for Marsha. She was certain that things just were not going to change. Anger, frustration, and determination began to well up inside me. I thought, *I'll show her! I can do this! God can do this! We will change!* Of course, I took some of what Marsha had to say personally; but more than feeling hurt, I felt embarrassed for God.

"God, don't these folks believe that you can do something about their situation?" I prayed. "Where is their faith? What about their trust?"

For months I experienced the hardening nature of disbelief—not just Marsha's disbelief but mine. Soon my optimism turned into frustration, and I began to argue with God: "Is this all you are giving me to work with? What am I supposed to do with people who don't want to change? Are you sure I am supposed to stay here?"

I felt pretty self-righteous in my anger, but I quickly realized I was not angry with the people. No, I was angry with God! I wanted different circumstances—a different setting—but all I could see was dry bones.

When Ezekiel had his vision in the valley of dry bones, he too did not see much hope. When asked, "Can these bones live?" he replied (perhaps with a hint of sarcasm), "Lord, you alone know." I totally can relate to that response! I would have said it this way: "I do not know if it is possible, God. You know everything, so you tell me: is it possible for these people to change?" In the middle of a vast valley of death, Ezekiel could not see what God saw—the possibility for new life. Honestly, neither could I.

I needed God to open my eyes and help me see the potential in the seemingly dry bones in front of me. I also needed to see the dryness in my own life. "Those people" were not the only ones experiencing spiritual death. I was missing one key ingredient to spiritual revitalization—the very breath of God. No matter how determined, strategic, and focused I was in changing the church's culture, I was wasting my time without the breath of God, the Holy Spirit.

The funny thing about the movement of the Spirit is that it doesn't just transform the people around us; it transforms *us*. We have to change too. I needed God to help me see what God saw in the people around me.

Instead of seeing the Marshas of the world as dry bones, I began to see them as children of God—people with a holy purpose. I began to believe that God was going to raise up a spiritual army in our church, and that God would use the Marshas of the church to do it. That's just what happened, and in the process God opened my eyes to the power of the Holy Spirit in the lives of everyone.

Can these dry bones live? You bet they can!

God, pour out your Holy Spirit on us—on me. Even though I see a valley of dry bones, open my eyes and heart to the potential of new life. Help me to name everyone I encounter "child of God" instead of dry bones; in Jesus' name. Amen.

17. Speak Life

So I prophesied as I was commanded. And as I was prophesying, there was a noise, a rattling sound, and the bones came together, bone to bone. (Ezekiel 37:7 NIV)

Sometimes I try to be prophetic. I want to speak the truth. But when the truth is not paired with love, it can sting a little.

One Sunday afternoon, the senior pastor and I were preparing for a church visioning meeting, and we decided to speak the truth—though I am uncertain how much love was in it. We wanted the people to wake up and realize just how seriously in trouble the church was. With my amateur editing skills, I altered a picture of the church sign to read "Closed," and we projected it onto a big screen. Then came the speech: "If you, you, you … don't, don't, don't … we will die, die, die."

There are times when God is asking us to speak the truth, but always it should be spoken in the context of love. I forgot that part. The visioning meeting was not a disaster, but there was some finger pointing and blame. Quickly I realized that if we were going to experience new life, it was not going to be the result of focusing on the problem. What we needed were solutions.

I began to ask myself this question: *What do you see?* There were some really fantastic people in the church, and they had beautiful gifts. What if I focused what I said—prophetically— on what they could do well instead of on what was not happening? What if I spoke life into the people instead of death? That's exactly what God was asking Ezekiel to do—to speak life into those dead bones.

I had been so focused on naming the problem that it had blinded me to the solution that was right in front of my face: the people. People are God's greatest resource. As I began to speak life into the beautiful gifts that people had and were using in the church, we began to experience change. I changed, and the people changed as a result.

Our words matter. Through the power of the Holy Spirit, they have the ability to bring *life*. My words changed from "We are dying people" to words such as this: "What if, Donna, you make that delicious bundt cake you make for every carry-in dinner and take it to the kids at the local homeless shelter? I know they would enjoy it. I know I do! And while we are there, we will play some games and talk with their parents." These words gave Donna purpose, but they also changed my perspective. The more I spoke life, the more we believed; and the more we believed, the more I spoke.

Words are powerful. It may sound silly to say that vocabulary plays such an important part in bringing renewed life, but it's true. So each day I think about how I am speaking the truth in love into the people around me: my spouse, kids, friends, neighbors, and even the strangers I meet.

Just as God challenged Ezekiel, God is challenging us to speak life into death. Today, speak life!

Jesus, open my mouth to speak life into circumstances. Challenge me not only to name the problem but to speak life into the situation and solution; in Jesus' name. Amen.

18. Unexpected Gifts

*The angel answered, "The Holy Spirit will come on you,
and the power of the Most High will overshadow you.
So the holy one to be born will be called the Son of God.
Even Elizabeth your relative is going to have a child in
her old age, and she who was said to be unable to conceive
is in her sixth month. For no word from God will ever
fail." (Luke 1:35-37 NIV)*

Donna surprised me one Sunday morning with an unexpected gift: a handmade tree skirt. The skirt was beautiful—white with red trim. Most folks would be thrilled to have a gift made with such care and love, but I was not. You see, a few weeks prior I had preached a message about a different tree skirt, one that I had wanted to purchase from a home improvement store. When my husband saw that it cost forty dollars, I quickly defended myself with, "But honey, I need it."

The truth is that I didn't need that tree skirt; I wanted it. So I didn't purchase it. In my sermon I railed against the effects of consumerism on our faith, particularly during the Advent season. I thought my message had been clear: we in the church do not need more stuff; we need more of Jesus.

But Donna was proud of her gift, so I politely accepted it and took it home with me. What I didn't yet realize was the unexpected gift that tree skirt would reveal.

When I was able to get over myself—over my interpretation of my sermon—God revealed to me that Donna's gift had nothing to do with the sermon. She did not misinterpret what I had said. She simply was being obedient to what God had asked her to do. At first I did not see the real gift, but God used that tree skirt to start a spiritual revolution within me. Through the movement of the Holy Spirit, God began to whisper to me, "Look right in front of your face, Rachel. These people are the gift." They were the ones God was using to reach the community, their peers, and even strangers. I had a preconceived notion of what transformation would look like, and God ignited a spiritual fire through the most unexpected of gifts.

That's what God did by sending Jesus. Jesus was not the gift that the people expected God to give. They expected a king, a political leader, a military genius, perhaps, but not a baby wrapped in swaddling cloths and lying in a manger.

So often I think that I need stuff—more resources, more training, more people, more money—to do the next big "God thing," but every day God reminds me, "Look at the unexpected gifts right in front of your face." As we saw in yesterday's devotion, people are God's greatest resource; and this Advent season I am reminded that God is calling me to pour my life into people so that they can pour their lives into others.

Donna had gifts that she freely shared with me and the rest of the world. Her handmade tree skirt opened my eyes to the simple but powerful gifts that she had to offer the church and the Kingdom. It also revealed to me that the gift of Jesus Christ comes in all forms, including a tree skirt.

I didn't need that forty-dollar tree skirt, but I certainly needed the handmade one.

Jesus, open my heart and hands to unexpected gifts. Help me to recognize that your gifts come wrapped in so many ways. Challenge me to use my gifts—and to encourage others to use their gifts—to reveal your Kingdom; in Jesus' name. Amen.

19. Bigger and Better?

Therefore, if anyone is in Christ, the new creation has come: The old has gone, the new is here!
(2 Corinthians 5:17 NIV)

The Advent and Christmas season can be chaotic and extremely busy. Sometimes I find myself repeating the mantra, "I don't want to survive; I want to thrive." It's easy for clergy types like myself to point fingers and place blame on the culture of consumerism that pervades nearly every aspect of the countdown to December 25. There are some really great reasons for this: Black Friday now starts on Thanksgiving Day, and the weekend is partnered with Small Business Saturday and capped off by Cyber Monday. As if that isn't bad enough, everything in the world seems to be on sale—from phones to produce to cars. It's a great time not only to purchase Christmas gifts but also to buy something bigger and better!

In our attempts to drown out the culture's consumerism, the church offers its own brand of busyness: Christmas plays, live Nativities, caroling, and multiple Christmas Eve services. Rather than transforming the lives of people, the church adds to the busyness and chaos. Advent becomes a practice of survival and endurance. Our purpose in the church is to prepare people for new life. But when church becomes one more thing added to a month of many things, the result is people who are exhausted, parched, and dry from their experience of preparation. This is not our calling. We do not need more programs; we need purpose!

Purpose is not found in doing one more big thing for God. How many times have you caught yourself saying, "Let's make Christmas even bigger and better this year?" That's impossible. The biggest, best Christmas has already happened, and everything we offer our friends, family, and churches is a mere glimpse of God's bigness. So instead of bigger and better, what if we tried new—not a new activity, but space for God to make *us* new. When we said yes to Jesus, Jesus said yes to making us new. Yet often we do not feel or experience "the new" because we are not allowing space for God to do the work.

This Advent God is asking us to offer ourselves, not because we are a big deal but because that's all God really wants. Following Jesus means surrendering our whole lives to God. And this season of preparation is the perfect time for God to breathe new life into us.

Do you want to survive or thrive this Advent and Christmas season? What space are you carving out of your everyday life to give God room to make you new?

Giver of new life, help me to allow the time and space in my calendar and my life so that all things can be made new. I offer my whole life to you. Breathe into me the life-giving wind of the Holy Spirit and make me new; in Jesus' name. Amen.

20. The Best Parties

"The servant came back and reported this to his master.
Then the owner of the house became angry and ordered
his servant, 'Go out quickly into the streets and alleys of
the town and bring in the poor, the crippled, the blind
and the lame.'" (Luke 14:21 NIV)

"I haven't had a home-cooked meal for Thanksgiving for
years! It would be nice to eat something that someone made
from scratch."

These were the words of Nate, one of a group of guys
who happened to be homeless and were hanging out with
me and some friends from seminary. We were weeks away
from Thanksgiving, and my husband, Jon, and I had planned
to celebrate with his parents and our daughter, Addie. This
would be our first Thanksgiving together since Addie's arrival.
Though grandparents can be reasonably territorial when it

comes to celebrating Thanksgiving with their first grandchild, Jon and I felt the nudge to extend our table.

We decided to prepare a family style Thanksgiving Day meal for our friends who happened to be homeless; and they wanted to be part of the planning. Nate, Bill, Franky, and the others began to make plans for the food they wanted to eat and the friends they, too, wanted to invite.

"Make sure Mrs. Donna makes a pecan pie."

"I'll help cook the turkey if someone can get me a ride."

"We've got friends all around town who want to come. Can we get a van to pick them up?"

Invitations went out to friends around town, as well as to people at the seminary who happened to be without family the week of Thanksgiving.

Then there was the matter of breaking the news to Jon's parents. It went something like this: "Steve and Betty, this year instead of having Thanksgiving with just 'our four and no more,' we are extending the table and throwing a party. And actually, we need your help. Steve, do you mind riding in the van with me as I pick up people from around town? And Betty, can you watch Addie as we get things ready for our meal?"

Of course, they had questions: "Do you have to do this on Thanksgiving Day? Why not some other day of the week? Isn't Thanksgiving Day for families?"

Our reply: "We *are* family."

Jesus challenges us with his table manners; he creates with his table a new way of being community—of being family. Here in Luke, he shares a story of a banquet. Although there are designated guests, they don't show up. The party planner asks a helper to go out and get a whole lot of people that most wouldn't invite. Even after that invitation, there is still room.

From Thanksgiving to Christmas, I quickly can become focused on my own biological family and forget that I am surrounded by folks who are looking to be part of something bigger—who are looking for family. Nate, Bill, Franky and many others are not blood relations, nor did they marry into the family, but they said yes to Jesus. They were and are part of the family of God.

I am challenged by Jesus to extend challenging invitations—and to throw the best parties! Jesus likes to party, and I want to be known as a person who knows how to throw a great party where everyone feels welcome—particularly those on the margins.

How can you extend your table to those who find themselves without family this season?

Generous Jesus, you extend your table to all. Grant me the grace and capacity to throw the best parities and, in doing so, to redefine what it means to be part of the family of God; in Jesus' name. Amen.

WEEK FIVE

JESUS CHANGES EVERYTHING

Jorge Acevedo

21. Glorious and Beautiful

Make sacred garments for Aaron that are glorious and beautiful. (Exodus 28:2 NLT)

In the Book of Exodus, God is very specific about the details of worship for the wandering Hebrews. The instructions regarding the portable worship center have been established, and now God turns his attention to the leaders or priests who will guide the people in their worship. The principle that the priests' sacred garments are to be glorious and beautiful guides every detail that follows. Because the God they were worshiping is glorious and beautiful, their clothing and behavior needed to follow.

In our day of casual attire in worship, the distinguishing "marks" of a cleric or pastor have been all but lost. Some would argue that this is a bad thing. Like the priests' garments in Exodus, the clerical collar or robe helps to "set apart" ministers and religious leaders. Others would argue that this "set apart" stuff hinders the priesthood of all believers.

I'm not sure who is right. I have chosen the more casual way, not necessarily for theological reasons but for comfort. But I do find it ironic that if church people ever do see me wearing a suit, I get lots of comments—from "Boy, you clean up well!" to "Wow, you should do this more often!"

When I view Exodus 28:2 from a "new covenant" perspective, I remember that Jesus is our high priest. One commentator wrote that the glorious and beautiful priestly garment in this verse reflects Jesus' glory and beauty, which he took off when he came to bring salvation to the earth.

Now let's make it personal. We are challenged by Romans 13:14 to "clothe yourself with the presence of the Lord Jesus Christ" (NLT). And in Galatians 3:27, Paul reminds us, "All who have been united with Christ in baptism have put on Christ, like putting on new clothes" (NLT). When we put on Jesus, we put on his glory and beauty.

Any glory and beauty in our lives comes from the One who took off his glory and beauty so that he could rescue and heal this sin-sick planet. Any glory and beauty in our lives is because of Jesus' glory and beauty shining through our brokenness. Today and throughout this season of Advent, let his glory and beauty shine!

Glorious and beautiful Lord, shine through my life today, revealing your glory and beauty. Amen.

22. The Unfinished Task

"For the Good News must first be preached to all nations." (Mark 13:10 NLT)

After Jesus foretold the destruction of the Temple in Jerusalem, four of the disciples came to him and asked, "When is this going to happen?" They were sitting on the slope of the Mount of Olives outside of Jerusalem. I've been privileged to stand on that very slope where Jesus looked at the city of David as he instructed his disciples.

In response to their question, Jesus began a long teaching that, frankly, I don't fully understand. But embedded in the middle of this diatribe on the signs of the end times, Jesus makes the statement that we find in today's verse. Its meaning is crystal clear, needing no historical or cultural context for interpretation. It simply communicates the reality that before the end, the gospel—the good news—must be accessible to all nations.

In this verse, the word *nations* is the Greek word *ethne,* from which we get the word *ethnic.* It means "people groups." Rather than referring to geographic boundaries, as we tend to think of nations, it is more contextual and local. God cares about people where they are and where they live. God desires for his radical grace to be expressed to every person on the planet in ways that are appropriate to where they are and where they live.

How appropriate that as I write this, I am in the nation called India, which has the largest numbers of *ethne* that still do not have access to the gospel. Yesterday as I heard the ministry staff here making their presentation, I was again impressed at how seriously and literally they take this mandate of Jesus. The gospel *must be* preached to all people groups first. Then the end will come.

The task is still unfinished. You and I are sent out—into our communities, our workplaces, and the world—to help the task be completed. Throughout this season and every day to come, let us share the good news of Jesus everywhere we are sent.

God, help me to join you in reaching the many ethne of your world. May I help advance the gospel today wherever you send me; to your glory and the fame of your name. Amen.

23. God's Will Can Be Messy

[Paul] said, "Why all this weeping? You are breaking my heart! I am ready not only to be jailed at Jerusalem but even to die for the sake of the Lord Jesus."
(Acts 21:13 NLT)

That night the Lord appeared to Paul and said, "Be encouraged, Paul. Just as you have been a witness to me here in Jerusalem, you must preach the Good News in Rome as well." (Acts 23:11 NLT)

Tracing Paul's journey from the mission field to Jerusalem, where he was imprisoned, and then eventually to Rome is quite an adventure. I'm captured by the two prophecies in Acts 21 where Paul was told not to go to Jerusalem because it would be his demise. Others saw the possible suffering he would endure as antithetical to God's will, yet Paul saw it as part of God's plan.

After his arrest, Paul got a word from Jesus. Jesus offered encouragement that the suffering would not be an end in itself but a means to a greater Kingdom end. Paul would indeed suffer on his journey to Rome, but Jesus would open doors for the gospel to be proclaimed. Sometimes God's will can be messy.

I was unintentionally taught to view God's will as a straight, linear experience. One metaphor to describe this view is guardrails on the highway that move us back to the center when we bump up against them. Phrases such as "the only place to live is in the center of God's will" are the mantra for this view. I understand the intent of that phrase. Living squarely in God's will preaches well and, frankly, easily. Our job is simply to discern God's will and stay in it.

That sounds good, but Paul's understanding of God's will was different. In fact, his understanding was antithetical to a group of faithful followers of Jesus who said, "Don't go to Jerusalem. You'll suffer." Paul responded, "I must go and suffer."

This first-century witness reminds me that God's will is difficult to discern. The other faithful followers of Jesus saw suffering as something to be avoided, but Paul saw suffering as something to be embraced. Remember, this was the guy who wrote, "I want to know Christ and experience the mighty power that raised him from the dead. I want to suffer with him, sharing in his death, so that one way or another I will experience the resurrection from the dead!" (Philippians 3:10-11 NLT). Paul embraced suffering with Christ as an honor and a privilege.

In our Western, pain-free Christianity, our tendency is to put space between suffering and God's will—as Paul's well-intentioned friends did. Perhaps we need to discern God's will more according to the development of personal character and the furthering of God's kingdom. Perhaps God's will is like two lenses in binoculars, with one lens being our personal, Christlike development and the other lens being God's kingdom expansion.

If suffering grows me and pushes the Kingdom ball up the hill, then I'm where I need to be. There are many life experiences I never would have asked God for, including a difficult journey with a family member's addiction and mental illness, but I know I am more completely God's and more fruitful for God's mission because of it. The will of God can be messy, but pursuing it is essential—even if it leads to suffering.

Advent may not be a time when we typically think about suffering, but consider this: Jesus came to earth and was willing to suffer for our sake and the fulfillment of God's plan. May we follow his example.

Lord, continue to grow my character and ministry to glorify you and expand your Kingdom. If suffering does this, then I welcome it. Help me to be sensitive to the whisper of your Spirit as I walk with Jesus today. Amen.

24. Ministry That Is Hidden

*I also devoted myself to working on the wall and refused
to acquire any land. And I required all my servants to
spend time working on the wall. I asked for nothing, even
though I regularly fed 150 Jewish officials at my table,
besides all the visitors from other lands! The provisions
I paid for each day included one ox, six choice sheep or
goats, and a large number of poultry. And every ten
days we needed a large supply of all kinds of wine.
Yet I refused to claim the governor's food allowance
because the people already carried a heavy burden.
Remember, O my God, all that I have done for these
people, and bless me for it. (Nehemiah 5:16-19 NLT)*

Nehemiah was in charge of rebuilding the wall around the
city of Jerusalem, a job that took fifty-two days in all. As he
led the people on the last twenty-six days of the building project, the inevitable pushback became even more pronounced.

(Evil seems to rage the closer a Kingdom assignment gets to fulfillment.) The letter writing, gossip, accusations, and even injustices among the people were all distractions for Nehemiah and his team's completion of the wall.

In verses 16-19, Nehemiah reported his selfless leadership activity, describing what he did that he did not have to do and what he did not have to do that he did. Reading these verses is like taking a look behind a righteous leader's activity. He ends this self-report with a short prayer, saying essentially, "God, you saw what I have done. Honor me for it." What is going on here?

Years ago I heard John Maxwell say, "Leaders die with secrets." He meant that when you seek to lead honorably, you will know things that you cannot share publicly that might shift public opinion your way. It's information that fills in gaps and clarifies things, but you cannot share it for a whole host of reasons. But in Nehemiah's story, his self-report was not about him having "insider information" about Sanballat or Tobiah—two of his opponents—that would clear his name or defend his assignment. It was more about the secret character of a righteous leader.

What is a righteous leader? It's one who quietly and unassumingly tithes and gives offerings. It's one who, under the cloak of darkness, works late into the night to prepare a lesson or write a message. It's one who visits a dying person at a hospice house because the person has no family and will otherwise die alone. It's one who answers a myriad of "emergency" phone calls and e-mails on a much-deserved and much-needed day off. It's one who, year after year, refuses the perks that he or she has earned for the greater good of the ministry budget. These are some of the seldom seen and often unnoticed assignments of a God-honoring leader.

I understand Nehemiah's prayer. He wanted God to know that God's recognition really mattered to him. "Please tell me you're seeing this, God" is often the prayer of a dedicated leader—a selfless servant of God—who does many things in relative obscurity. It's an appropriate prayer for *all* of us. After all, we're all called to be dedicated servants of Jesus Christ, sent to be his hands and feet in the world.

This Advent may we find unseen ways to minister to others, and may our prayer be that of Nehemiah, asking that God alone sees and is pleased.

Lord, I'm not always like Nehemiah. Far too often my heart and mind drift toward a "what's in it for me" attitude. I battle with comparison, wrestle with envy, and jockey for prominence. Thank you for the ways you are wrenching these desires from me. Give me the capacity of your Spirit to do ministry that is hidden. May my right hand not know what my left hand is doing. My desire is to serve and please you alone; all for your glory, God. Amen.

25. Affection, Not Activity

"When you produce much fruit, you are my true disciples. This brings great glory to my Father." (John 15:8 NLT)

Jesus is teaching his disciples in the Upper Room about the necessity of staying intimately connected to him. The Father tends the garden. Jesus is the vine. The Holy Spirit is the sap. The collective "you" are the people of God—that includes us—who together produce much fruit. Notice it doesn't just say fruit but "much fruit"—a bumper crop, the maximum harvest. All this glorifies the Gardener, the Father.

Jesus never defines what this "much fruit" is. Preacher types like me want to make this about church activity, and I'd imagine there is some truth in that. As collective followers of Jesus—also called the church—we pray, pay, and plan for activity that glorifies the Father and helps people. From Sunday worship to Saturday outreach events, we seek to do

God's bidding. But I wonder if Jesus had something completely different in mind.

The very next thing Jesus says is that we are supposed to remain in his love. Then he says: "This is my commandment: Love each other in the same way I have loved you. There is no greater love than to lay down one's life for one's friends" (John 15:12-13 NLT). Could Jesus mean that our collective "much fruit" is our collective sacrificial love for one another?

We want to make the "much fruit" about activity when it seems that for Jesus it was about affection. Love for one another defines, refines, and identifies us as God's people. Activity without affection is sheer drudgery anyhow. It's joyless.

Several years ago, a server at a national chain restaurant commended our men's small group for meeting there every Wednesday morning. Just our faithful gathering together for study, encouragement, and support was a witness of Christ's love. That is "much fruit."

What is the "much fruit" in your life? How is God calling you to join others in sharing Christ's love?

Lord, help me to join your people in your love revolution on this planet. As we are sent and we serve together, may it splash out of us onto everyone we meet. Forgive me for making fruit-bearing an individualistic thing when you intend it to be a collective demonstration of our sacrificial love. May the truth that your love changes everything revolutionize our world! Amen.

ABOUT THE AUTHORS

(L to R) Justin LaRosa, Rachel Billups, Jorge Acevedo, Lanecia Rouse, Jacob Armstrong

Jorge Acevedo is the lead pastor at Grace Church, a multi-site United Methodist congregation in Southwest Florida. He is the author of *Vital: Churches Changing Communities and the World,* coauthor of *The Heart of Youth Ministry,* and has been a contributor to *Circuit Rider* magazine, *Good News* magazine, and *Our Faith Today.*

Jacob Armstrong is the founding pastor of Providence Church, a five-year-old United Methodist church plant in Mt. Juliet, Tennessee, reaching one thousand people each week. Providence's vision is to see those who are disconnected from God and the church find hope, healing, and wholeness in Jesus Christ. Jacob is the author of *Treasure: A Stewardship Program on Faith and Money; The God Story: Seven-Week Sermon Series; Upside Down: A Different Way to Live; Loving Large: Four-Week Sermon Series; Interruptions: A 40-Day Journey with Jesus;* and *The New Adapters: Shaping Ideas to Fit Your Congregation.*

Lanecia Rouse is the author of numerous articles on Christian formation for Upper Room Ministries and Abingdon Press. She has held pastoral roles in The United Methodist and the British Methodist Church, most recently as project manager of The Art Project, Houston, a therapeutic art ministry with those experiencing homelessness. Lanecia earned a bachelor's degree in sociology from Wofford College and a master of divinity degree from Duke Divinity School. She currently lives in Houston, where she continues her ministry as a writer, artist, photographer, and workshop leader.

Justin LaRosa is a licensed clinical social worker and deacon who leads the new ministry of Hyde Park United Methodist Church in downtown Tampa, Florida. He served for eight years as the minister of discipleship, working with a team of leaders to facilitate the process of organizing, training, empowering, and supporting laypersons. Justin is coauthor, with James A. Harnish, of *A Disciple's Path* and *A Disciple's Heart.*

Rachel Billups serves as the executive pastor of discipleship and as part of the preaching team for Ginghamsburg Church in Tipp City, Ohio. Rachel, an ordained elder within The United Methodist Church, holds a bachelor's degree in Bible/Religion and History from Anderson University and a master of divinity degree from Duke Divinity School. Before joining the Ginghamsburg team, Rachel served as the lead pastor of Shiloh United Methodist Church, a multi-site church in Cincinnati, Ohio.

CPSIA information can be obtained
at www.ICGtesting.com
Printed in the USA
LVHW08s1521290918
591773LV00003B/3/P